SHAM CITY

SHAM
CITY

EVAN HARRISON

OMNIDAWN PUBLISHING

RICHMOND, CALIFORNIA

2012

Cover photographs by Taryn Cowart

Cover and Interior Design by Cassandra Smith

Typefaces: Minion Pro and Gil Sans Std
Printed on Finch 60# Recycled 30% PCW Natural Opaque Vellum

Library of Congress Cataloging-in-Publication Data

Harrison, Evan Samuel, 1984-
Sham city / Evan Harrison.
p. cm.
Poems.
ISBN 978-1-890650-63-6 (trade pbk. : alk. paper)
I. Title.
PS3608.A78344S53 2012
811'.6--dc22
2011051413

Published by Omnidawn Publishing, Richmond, California
www.omnidawn.com   (510) 237-5472   (800) 792-4957
10 9 8 7 6 5 4 3 2 1
ISBN: 978-1-890650-63-6

The author would like to thank the editors and staff of the following journals, in which some of the poems in this book previously appeared: alice blue, Bat City Review, CutBank, DIAGRAM, Hayden's Ferry Review, Otoliths, and Product.

ONE

SHAM LIFE

The adversary lies on the ground
because he sleeps stuffed with rubies and corn

The entire plain is a shadow

I began to sweat amid the cheering

A village drowns in the sweet contents
of its privatized wells

Because I want to be chagrined
when my hands catch on fire

For all these appliances in streams of silver
I need an outlet

For all these white horses and cut-outs
I need a press pass

And because the adversary sleeps stuffed with diamonds and flour
the horse just once bucks

Sham City

This tree is really something in a row with other trees the space between each roughly equal. Runny boulevards. The business park is a labeled organ and each pest is a scalpel. Elsewhere fluids suck bedness from the walkways cloud-gists pump across the Quik Stop window. Where to go. What is cheap. A lit-up spoon and bowl emporium retrofitted with cracking chairs from the weedy railside. The screen secondarily serving as mirror removes typical revulsion. Jams of paper and traffic and blood and raspberries. The man basks on a dusty wave prepared to lose it.

SHAM EVENING

Cool cool sundown era: a bat of drama
and the stray's bonfire eyes.
Hi there. The parking deck is a large sad man.
To never say these things.
For damages resulting from sundown
the state awards hot rice, greasy meat.
A hawk slaps the ground.
Most buildings and living things are exteriors.
A heathen of laughter. A roach of balance.
Bye there. That pigeon is a goner.
> A pigeon of choices.
> A pigeon's coal eyes.
> Cold dark era.

SHAM COUNTRY

Some feathered quiver. Most sleep.
Great spools of cable, a lowing unsourced.

At times the tension towers evoke "marvelous horror,"
their swath a blown-up furrow, an agriculture.
Most sleep. Most chairs overturned in nominal light.

One dream features the known faceless in a fluorescent
basement with proliferating corners. Rains have beat
the mud up onto the ground-level windows, fixation.

Everything processional. Moths corner the motel
ice machine, the breezeway suffers factory air.

The only machines forever rest.
Bloated low-flying craft respond to one blink
repeated to whole minds of houses. Enter the toad
        in unfortunate water.

Sham Mollusk

Sometimes all melody is dirty
alone with all that pearl

as the gas billows white
in a cracking present. Recede
is to the shelled valley as to the borders,

all those ribbons of color and kelp,
those pant legs blown to ribbons.

Listen to the tissue fold. Sands hum.
Sometimes salt rattling in the coffer, salt

accidentally getting on
the treasured tongue.

How to sight read in the clasped dark?

ADVICE FROM A HEAD

Buy lowly in a feed of grace it's said,
sell highly blind and ruby-throated.

Determine loosely enough for the search.
Justify use under the following bridge

to the conquered inland. It goes:
hope little. Use the serrated one for that.

Diversify in the bald patch of some copse
you manage to figure. Really stop cleaning the glass.

Deposit a theory in the gutter, bank or mud.
Haunt that choice. Invest in a voice

from the satellitic clutter and cordon
every hint of longing tenor. Crook and bumble.

Quick tip: exscrounge. Withdraw a monolith, bury it
on paper, so the digger gets dirty and in falls straight.

COLLECTIVE PUNISHMENT

You make the desert in my heart bloom
is all wrong now.
A white pest coherently reproducing in the grove.

You look nice today.
Only today

stopped speaking
to fill it in. A blue bird remotely guided
toward a hive of grainy figures.

Look, let's have

a casual dinner.
Ending at the car glowing at night.

Bloom
as one end of scope in another world
from the other.

You suck air from my lungs like a Hellfire missile.

THE COMMON COLD

I have a last leg. Say good times
are the edge of first dark.
Do so many years and a person
gets a new head, in a way.
May be a last good year.
The way a person has new doubts.
The first law says time the world
until sleep. Don't find a way.
Last year, he said only truths and
in that way, he was not a good person.
Time doesn't have a big plate.
His new tooth flew first.
Do you have a new way
to be good? The last time,
people said little. Every year I think
of my first breath and wince.

The world makes its own
man. A little thing goes—
herein the great project gets vicious.
I've known a day too long.
Day flashes its great thing lovingly
to make men cover their faces.
Go ahead, get the long respect
to know your little own world.
Get your own things in that long line.
A great day to know some cons.
A man goes to the floor
as the world makes a little tick.
The great man makes sweat
for a day, his own little river.
This long world gets to know me
just as I go with my things.

Think like the child.
See the other big shadows come
to parts in your right choice.
Life takes its old hand rudely.
Part of the prognosis is right.
See other life come to the big table
as the hand thinks what's right.
Take this old child.
The right path takes big hands,
but a part comes to not think.
The old books persist in moth life.
See the child as the other mistake.
I thought to grow old, for that child
to come see the right failure.
To take a life means other things.
Give her a big hand, a difficult part.

This work looks like high dread.
Give the eye's use a large revision,
use some different engine of want.
Small place for the woman.
Give the work a high estimated value
or small grudge. A woman looks
at the large spread of places.
She wants to use a different eye.
I want to give one eye to the large
farms to use a different approach.
Women at work look to the high
lungs, a place for small plots.
From high places of no work
the woman wants a large favor.
My eye gives small returns.
She uses a different organ to look.

All week I found important notes.
The government works today, in case.
A young fool asked for the next point
and I told it to wake up early.
If asked, some young work
for the government. Next week they'll find
bare rooms. A cop tells me an important point:
it's too early to pick up a case.
Ask to work and you find webs.
It's early for the next case.
An important week for the young
government, its point told.
The work week young, I found
the next important case.
Now I'll tell the government early
prey asks for a point.

Public parks leave a few problems.
A number of trustees seem depressed.
The company feels bad for trying
to put warring peoples in the same group.
I left that bad company to try feeling
less. A few groups seem effective
in handling these problems. The number
of public sheddings remains the same.
The public feels shame over its group
consciousness. I seem bad or inessential
to a number of companies. A few try
leaving for the same spiritual problems.
Leave the company to try cultivating
public problems. The number of disasters
seems the same as always.
Few apes feel bad for the group.

Preview

The report, to be issued tomorrow, will gore free association and stink of digging. The words *demarcation, furthermore,* and *course* will appear multiple times without gesturing toward notions of languish. The report will continue to make me feel poorly about the way I conduct my life, but some adults may go buy a magnet or regard gut, spectral strains of words as gospel or serious business. We will move deliberately in our mirrors as if filmed, as if the report were a script, safe, lumbering in artificial recesses. Translators on other continents will spend a lousy dawn. The subsequent media exegesis will raise flounder, resort to graphics and crow upon the wire of a letter. The pages will be ochre to those with certain corneal damages. Notably absent, peregrination of a particular fingertip in manufacturing undershirts, patterns of moss, an uninhabited space.

DESPOT / LEVIATHAN

This rifle came from a sweaty fire. For dark glasses, for tassels, for browned bird. My bicep is a whale on inebriated seas. So there is rattle at the border. Does this sleek metal quiver? Does the paint job wince? I will huff into my cell. These pectorals are premium steaks, grandiose livers peppered with fine workers. I drink honeyouckle champagne horseback. Privacy is political. I have a back of highlands. I know our national stomach is volcanic, so the quartet plays something familiar like gold. This rifle will come to the banquet warm. I am tenacious, fit for the clingy magazines and clingy dreams.

Getting Clean

I can appreciate a warm bath
lathered with shadows of UAVs.

In a warm bath I think about the economy
of showers and the rationale of my tired flesh.

In a shower I don't think about my tired flesh
outside of myself splashed about the courtyard.

I can appreciate good heat and then shower;
a sudden ball of light is the sun.

THE CALENDAR

The fastidious planner wracks her desk. Each day
in relation to the previous day. Plenty of terms
flipping like ivory cards.
  In the future perfect, wildfires converge
or we stop keeping in touch. Comping, passé, harmonious.
The lizard lowers to scuttle. The security
cavalcade trundles forlornly. Each hour pushing
into its far numbers. Few branches left to crack
loose in our overhead.
  Little fires engendered in the future present.
Furtive, aleatory, unassuming. The lizard was just here.
A sourness two days old. Each day
prematurely doused. The pits play at odds.
Paste of ash and rainwater in the sinkhole. The lizard shades
for a second. A ladder slides back into the hood.
  Some minutes familiarly absent.
A single mallet to fling at the piano. A blaze lunges
for the final air. The lizard pushes up before his cardinal billow.

FILM SCHOOL

To haul lights across a muddy prairie.
That to study lament.

We studied lament. To shoot from the ditch.
To weed the frame to echo her stockings and mad search.

Without breathing down clocks to signal passage.
To melt the factory in the distance.

That to foreground a product. We grew shabby.
How a call decays. To bury a dummy in snow.

Without washing the streets of the living.
To make an actor work through smoke to leave his face.

Recession of the magic hour.
How most inventions are fables.

FIGURES WITH SCRAP AND ADDRESS

I.

The dead hare is unteachable, warmed in thick arms,
a funnel for hopes, perfect lump for cradle or frame.
A hive of cotton gently waving. White rippled hairs pitch
nests and crosses on my nice shirt.
      The slate exhibits months of a migration,
a neglected garden, chronic revision. I turn the chair.
Irregularities of gold, tin legs, orbits of loose pearls.
I toe the dented floor.
      As you move past, a slack heart of gauze
finds its tremor. The glass will not continue as such.
There is too much to spell. The checklist grown sallow,
paper too brittle for marks.
      The worry is the coyote, your skin if there,
the glazed assembly at the wooden antenna.

2.

The disk of wax is a mock sea of dry violet,
a keeping place for pins. Dust and fur will probably light,
and I will comment on your calendar, noncommittal
like the pliable ripple.
      The animal is perennial for a stretch of path
if the period comes to cold again. There is a broom
for a floor like that, and a spade. You have a door
that would serve as table.
      Frequently you stepped on the arrangement
of strings and rashly-lain columns. A ruin is the glut
of affection, if I understood. A hazard, in the way
the wall looses countries of itself.
      In shelves of rows, the jar is the recourse,
fogged and scratched, storing a black nest of matches.

3.

A wooden head is blank in eye, washed cream,
singing its red fist. The one slate emits loops of readings,
wormed traces on the sheet of copper, the nail retreating
from its only work.
     You nod loosely, the shadow a painting,
corner a home for the arresting fabric, the web
of state somehow brought in. A paper beetle resists,
a shell tremors, I resituate.
     If a lock functioned, the air would turn.
You haven't felt the wire's care, the gilded wood
and topography in oil. If a switch moved, we could end
the reenactment of a lecture.
     The penalty is the stare, the symmetrical visage,
the page of law and penciled blossoms.

4.

The spool is wound in rosy expiration,
a miniature table set with iron and screwed-up mice,
a piano up to here in dun plaster. A paw rises,
and my ear does a number.

      If I really heard it, if a spoken word had integrity
amid the vascular fuss, maybe we could get out
the placemats and stemware. The ceremony
might overbear, the courses gel.

      Breath cannot ground the mote, affluent
in guard. The border of thread looks wild
with lonely eaters. I draped our chest with that map
made in the quiet.

      White ringing, your mind changing,
two wooden wheels purring across stone.

5.

The quilt is folded and nailed atop the high shelf,
the hare patters in its spring, wedged with knowledge.
Bowled rubble, bad reception. I folded. I held it.
A figurine of the hand.
    I considered the cloudbank of black felt fraught
with a human form. I thought to stuff the bottles with scrapes
of fat. I was wrong, like that pool of stitching
or the import of leaves.
    Little designs like you may have done in boredom,
varieties of hair locked in a floor-bound nebula,
and you let the pigment find its way through the paper
into the figure of a lung.
    We put the torso upright, drew a window
on its back, and watched the paper boxes combust.

THREE

CATHEDRAL

What else is a cathedral?
Vertical emphasis is an effective show of power; it makes people enjoy
  the idea of a god in space.
It's also a design for stacking all those families and quiet, banished
  loners.
Sometimes when they go to the store they just buy toilet paper and a
  suitcase of beer.
A hawk living in her dome would think
we were all part of an upset lemon tree.
What else?
The light coming through a rose window is almost like a noise that
  resembles a phone conversation about a third party's
  imminent passing.
Gothic tracery reminds me that I am not among the first inhabitants
  of the world,
but if I were among the last, I'd pitch my tent under the facade of the
  Duomo di Milano.
I am thinking of the Soviet-era apartment buildings in Warsaw,
  of the volume inside and inside.

PARA EL OÍDO OSCURO DE VALLEJO

after "Heces"

It's a tar day, you wave a coma noon; carry no
tangled onus, devolve, voor, core a sun,

It's a tar day, a dual say. Poor can know a desire.
This day graced a pain; this day dab your hair.

It's a tar day in Lima, you waver. You're a quarter
lost, carve air as cruel as day, miss ingratitude;
may blackened day, a loose brace, hew a map
of mass fairly, say too "No solace, I see."

Missive lent as florescent egress; elaborate and
ignore, maybe dreaded; entrench or glance ill.
Upon the rail, silent odes on shuddering need
connote less came on to sell pounds of denial.

Poorest, it's a tar day, coma noon, convey
co-nesting bruises, co-nesting core a son.

The others pass on and even doom interest in
too many, pour quotidian
inhalant, rupturing already haunted, dull ore.

It's a tar day, you wave, you waver much. No
tangled onus, devolve, veer, core a sun.

APOLOGY

Tomorrow retrobloomed.

Each petal got dried sluggish
and scrawled away.

It happened I had orphaned the nucleus,
was a no-show—

I'm sorry, but it turned out pleasantly unsurgical.

The layer of seen, repeated
outward, derailed

so that no I could make it,
no bouquetish we—

a hand of roots unmoored,
pressed into a ream of translations:

what do you mean? becomes
a soil tunnel.

Keeping House

Carve news into the door,
bat tethers.
Scour the region
of consumptive displays.
Spew vinegars,
swing the mop.
Hallow the thinnest cans
and loosest shame.
Get dusting in the mire
of livings, get the cat away
from the plastic.
Rattle the halls,
divide the ashes.
Wake reservedly glad,
maybe thin by evening.
Stanch the vain hum.
Preheat. Wash heels.
Find a place for that part
and this part
given its shape.
Drag along the blinds,
flour the flames,
sledge the balking wall.
Curl up, welcome guests.
Wire the fence,
secure a hinge.

People Walk in a Row Wearing Masks

Face one:
>I understand our condition

Face two:
>Put country first with plastic cement

Face four:
>A matter of digging connectedly reading the right shit

Face six:
>Passionate about appraisal restoration shellac

Face seven:
>Fortune ate a worked-over slab

Face nine:
>Central Center Center

Face ten:
>Soul as effigy gestural hocked

Face eleven:
>Digital holdings as in fingers

Face twelve:
>I want a tangible image by which to remember

Face thirteen:
>Cusp mapping bone tossing

Face fourteen:
>Heartburn as lifestyle

Face fifteen:
>Husky analogies to chess

Face sixteen:
>I recommend the leather margins

Face seventeen:
   My car is like my first home
Face nineteen:
   Everything seduces
Face twenty:
   I get it

SUGGESTED PHRASES FOR THE IMMINENT MOMENT

all that glitters sputters
all the dictator's paraphernalia
all the horse's oaten laws
all lung and no tendon
all work and yes please
all hands on pipe
all ears swollen vegetal
all eyes popped upon the plain
all hell washed into the body
all bets are won in time
all the malt beverage in america
all your batteries in one clock
all along the apartheid wall
all aboard the bare axle
all the rage the affection

Hot Day

I've tried to rip hard wires
frothing nobility
in the refined pasture
the concourse as it may
I've strangled the fallen pony
a mercy of pollen
or chasm or channel
or blues and clouds or square foot tiles
whatever cows me
whatever engenders suction
suggests congress
I've feigned like an animal
summer's spare young
the floral cross
a fire of shoulders
I've made a mockery of each oasis
looping my arrivals
in feast and dismissal
it is finally magnificent

ALLOWANCE

Tell me about the full
volcanoes, their frost alarms,

favors of the course.
Explain low total vanity

or how purest applies
to lock. Tell me

how a mandible rocks
and ticks need deer.

The night is good for it,
humid muteness inviting.

Outline buds, riven casement,
recite the tablet's waltz,

the whole scaffold localized
in my capitulating posture.

In the Air

All is false is a dogfight,
work of brief fire and long smoke.

On the face of it
small victories register.

The mountain is superficial
through our capillary frame,

and the instruction of density
maintains surface renewal.

And now the blossom,
crushed metal.

And now the explosive
posits a fresh zenith.

Chalk it for posterity.
Act within the dome.

American Domestic Architecture

The intersecting gable bears down on the yard like an unseemly forehead. Forthwith the patriarchs line up to ram their heads on the clapboard.

Down from the projecting eaves rain silver wires of trouts. Why, the last tenant is split-legged over the steep pitched roof.

And why not? A lonely woman is hugging a splayed column, so sincere and desperately tender, but her brothers on the porch cannot stifle conjectures.

The front fascia board once read *heterodoxy*. A boy sees where the nailed letters were and thinks how some words remind him of other words.

Home, home, home. Squirrels and fleas wriggle colluding from the louvered vent and a sore in the northern cornice.

The house violates most codes, a distinction clearly noted on the inspector's clipboard.

On the southern ivied bank, mutts paw and pee on the historic blueprints.

The builders are long dead; their obituaries follow.

Evan Harrison lives in Hattiesburg, Mississippi. He graduated in 2011 from The Center for Writers at The University of Southern Mississippi.